Finches in Kilmainham

Finches in Kilmainham

poems

D. Walsh Gilbert

GRAYSON BOOKS
West Hartford, Connecticut
graysonbooks.com

Also by D. Walsh Gilbert

Ransom
Once the Earth had Two Moons
imagine the small bones
[M]AR[Y]
Deirdre

Acknowledgments

My sincere gratitude goes to those who courageously read these poems, including my Partners in Poetry workshop group, the Farmington Valley Chapter of the Connecticut Poetry Society, and especially, the first readers of this collection, Ginny Lowe Connors and Sherri Bedingfield, who encouraged me to continue writing this manuscript despite its dark nature. I give heartfelt recognition to Julia Morris Paul for the generosity of some shared words. And without question, this story would not have come together without the assistance of the poet and scholar, Matthew Shelton, University of California, Berkeley, and his extensive understanding of the Irish language and history.

My Irish essence emanates from my grandmother, Annie May McNally Brennan, who first told me her stories of the Ireland she left when just a young woman, and to my mother, Sarah Josephine Brennan Walsh, who sang all the old Irish songs. My heart belongs to them.

—DWG

Dedicated to the generations of my Irish family who went before me.
And so, we continue.

Contents

Irish Pronunciation Guide

Áine	AHN-yuh
An Gorta Mór	ahn GORE-ta MORE
Aoibheall	EE-val
Bealtaine	BELL-tuh-nuh
Bean sí	BAN shee
Boann	BŌ-an
Bodhrán	BŌ-rahn
Brideóg	BREE-jōg
Cailleach	CALL-yuhch (guttural ch)
Cian	KEE-an
Cipín	ki-PEEN
Clochán	CLAH-hawn (guttural h in hawn)
Connaught	CON-noct
Drogheda	DRAH-heh-dah (guttural first h in heh)
Fionn	FIN
Fomhórach	fah-MORE-eh
Gaol	JALE
Leanbhán	LYAN-uh-van
Lucht Siúl	lawcht shool (guttural ch)
Mac Giolla Bhríghde	mc Gill-uh VREE-juh
Mórrígan	MORE-ee-gun
Naomhóg	NEEV-ōg
Róisín	RŌ-sheen
Seosamh Mac Cathmhaoil	SHO-sav mc CAW-fee-ill
Siabhra	SHEE-vrah
Sidhe	SHEE
Spailpín	spoll-PEEN
Tearmann	CHYAR-uh-muhn
Triskele	tree-SKEEL
Uisneach	ISH-nock

Not a mutineer walks handcuff'd to jail but I am handcuff'd to him and walk by his side...
Not a youngster is taken for larceny but I go up too, and am tried and sentenced.

—Walt Whitman, *Song of Myself, 37*

The Great Hunger

An Gorta Mór.
And another mother lowers her dead infant
into a pit dug in the middle of night
so her neighbors won't be aware: *Hail Mary,*
as she falls to her knees, *Pray for us sinners.*
Now, and at the hour of our death. Amen.

Her bare feet split at the heel
with scuffs and cracks and blisters.
Mud-covered, ragged toenails, black toes,
festers, wounds at the ankles.
Men, women, children—together, but alone.

Calluses, boils, and rot to the marrow—
forced into hovel, into holes in the bog,
forced to eat nettle, limpet, seaweed, and grass.
Bury the dead without coffins and then,
try to catch the rats and the dogs.

Look at their soles, the Black Fever,
Road Fever—
when families lay down, together as one,
and succumb.

Some only stare at the tattered cuffs.
Some turn from the hair, from the teeth.
Some close their eyes. Some walk away.
Some are awake to the open-ground graves.
Some hear the prayers and say nothing.

Some will bring soup. Some stirabout porridge.
Starvation on old meat and cheap corn.
And skeletons continue to sharpen.

The specters and demons will speak
from the graves,
tattered and praying,
sour, ugly, and bleeding.
But the chaffinch in the hedge will keep singing,
its feet holding fast to what's green.

Ann Gallagher, Also Known as Dill

She's the delicacy of the lace of Carrickmacross
with petit point freckles on a complexion of milk,
mink-brown curls spindled and tatted,
                    the floss of a lamb in April.

She's string bean legs and buttery skin,
the smile of a candle at sundown. She's
the tan-linen tablecloth left on the clothesline,
a canvas the pins can't hold still:
                    the chatter of magpie,
                    an eavesdropping mouse,
                    the teeter of a three-legged fox.
She's turf-fire warming winter's clear rhinestone light,

and she's nicknamed Dill, a spicy weed,
an annual thought to be short-lasting.
She's the nestling abandoned in its manger straw
while the cat is climbing the limb.

The garda call her the spot on the cloth
left after Sunday's tea—the thumbprint, the sin
which can't be removed, no matter the soap,
the scrubbing, the rinse.
                    Yet, the more it's washed,

the more it softens, and she's the heirloom thread,
                    the fiber, the flax
                    left in the field to return.
Perennial.
She's the gentle blue flower who wouldn't be killed—
who stayed and scattered in mid-century wind

until its seeds could land
                on wrought, overturned earth.
And field stones heard the seeds taking root.

The Gallagher Family

So many routes on the famine roads—
Dill's baby brothers, once rosy-cheeked,
six, four, and just three years old,
were already gone in a scourge of measles.
Buried now by the peated lands,
three wooden crosses in unconsecrated ground.

Her mother knew the rash could take her daughters, too,
so she exiled Dill and big-sister Kate
to live in the pig shed—pig squeals long silent,
muck still wet.
The girls chased out the fur-raggedy cats
—flea-riddled and blind with infection—
cats who howled atop the roof:
the bean sí's wail of death.

Then, it wasn't too long with the flux
before her mother also lay dead.
Until her father himself would shroud his wife,
and huddle exhausted, starved, and fevered—
what had once been a man.

There had been hope when Dill's father
was 'getting the cool'—temporary improvement—
his fever down, his nose-bleeding stopped,
but his skin stayed yellow, and he kept retching
until nothing was left of him.

There had once been hope, but now there was none.
Relapsing fever: the curse of the poor.
Then, the dogs came, and the girls fled
as the landlord chuckled,

Extermination assistance. Her father
attacked, bitten—eaten alive.

So, Kate took Dill on the black famine road,
to Drogheda village, to its famous river, Boyne.

They were together until one was lost,
and one was left all alone.

Dill's Passage

1. Engine

Dill doesn't have shillings for fare, so she hops the train
— solo—Drogheda to Dublin town with its real-life castle

and two rivers: the Poddle and the Liffey. Her father
had blarneyed all about Dublin. Gold crowns! She imagines

princesses, a king and queen, a fairytale, and the limestone head
of St. Patrick himself carved onto the Chapel Royal.

Surely, the likes of them can find her elder sister, Kate,
gone off without her into a vast open land. Dill now left alone.

But no one explained that Dubh Linn means *black pool*,
and tall soldiers in tall hats ride tall horses.

No one explained that some of the Poddle flows water-hidden,
peat-stained, and dark underground—no cleansing well—

rather buried and clandestine as the workings of a prison.

2. Coach

The locomotive belches black smoke, and train wheels
claw the railroad ties the way a harrier locks talons
on a heathland grouse. Screeching for its life.
Dill believes this beast is alive: tremble, rumble, and breath.
But the Dublin & Drogheda Railway carries her
past Balbriggan, Skerries, Malahide, Baldoyle, and then
into Dublin. No one should notice one little girl tucked
in a passenger car going thirty miles an hour, hidden

between trunks, ladies' bonnets, and the canes of old men.
She clings to the fold of a mother's afternoon dress.

No one should notice—locomotive and smoke.
If the dragon doesn't eat her, she'll ride it to the end,
see the gray-granite station with its tall square tower,
then, hop off to search for her Kate.

3. Caboose

On arrival,
the peeler follows.
He had noticed.
Indeed.
He calls out,
Stowaway!
Thief!
Whistles
once, then twice,
and shouts,
Begging vagrant,
stinkin' imbecile,
when Dill lifts a parsnip
from a vendor's cart.
One wilting parsnip.
Until—his grasp on her arm.
That's how she'd go:
      Kilmainham Gaol.
      Five months.

Into Kilmainham's West Wing

Like the writhing serpents of hell itself, five stone heads
on five slithering bodies twist together
and transom the entry—five fearsome eyes, the pointed wings
of dragons, tongues and scaled skin, teeth filed and able to rip,

all collared and chained into tangle, all spiraled like a triskele
—here life, death, and rebirth in a wicked harmony.
Incarceration is a new existence for the peasant, poor, and hungry.

This doorway greets the prisoner: the felon, the debtor, the woman,
the child—thief of parsnip and train fare.
Once the black iron gates are unbolted and opened, the darkness

is broken only by a sick-green gaslight, then there's limestone
and granite, brick and thick walls, and a long, narrow corridor
girdered in rows of Victorian gingerbread—scrolled brackets,

curled iron—almost beautiful—like vines or the waves of the sea.
Are these the arabesque of turnabout and resurrection?
This is Gallows Hill. This is Kilmainham Gaol

with one candle for each cell and buckets of cold piss to slop out
each morning. Here, on dirt and stone slabs, the prayers
of the condemned—the murderer, rapist, and traitor.

     What's heard?
     A man crying for his mother.
     The footsteps of his jailer.
     An iron bolt as it slides through the jamb.
     The squeak of a rat and the scratch
       after lice
       and the fleas
     where a baby awakes on the floor.

The inmates hear
the jangle of keys, the jangle of those carved serpents' chains,
and the death bell which rings when the hanged bodies fall,
executions in full public view.

The Warden Adds One More

Drogheda's street gutter had been Connaught hard
whenever Dill lay caught in the rain—months

since she'd shrouded her mother with linen—with her
only skirt—and her apron had covered a brother.

Now, she's wearing her father's old trousers,
(God rest his soul) bone-ragged and ripped

at the knees from prayer and digging for spuds.
Pants rolled at her ankles are cinched

with flax rope at her waist, a narrow waist
wasted, wasting still, growl-begging

for a heel of bread, a sip of milk, then settling
for that Dublin parsnip—golden, stolen,

still clutched in her hand and not
to be denied when the lawman finally got her.

She knew she was falling, fallen surely,
—barefoot, lice-smitten, hair-matted, dun-smudged—
into manure and dogshit and an Englishman's spit.

But while the street's gutter had been Connaught hard,
the stones of Kilmainham are now harder yet
when the constable closes the oak door.

Inside, there's five of them, all children—skinny
and reeking, homeless and orphaned,
and the cell grows dark, and rainwater drips.

But a crust of bread
lays moldy for her in a dented tin-metal pan.

The Long Road Before

Dill believes
she sees Kate
in the cell
when a fringe
of dawn's light
burns through
the high window.
A whisper. A promise.

It lies to her.
She recognizes
none of these children—
a boy, two girls,
an elder teen, pregnant,
still sleeping
on straw and sackcloth.
Feverish breaths
warm and raspy.

Dill thinks she hears
Here. Come here.
But it's their haunting
expirations
wheezed
out of sync.
There is no Kate.

Her sister left her
on the River Boyne's bank,
left her
in raw March rain,
black as blight,
mean as salt

on an open wound.
She'd waited
and waited some more.

Kate had gone
to snitch a fishing line,
somewhere,
elsewhere, anywhere.
There were salmon
in this river:
her father's stories
of Fionn and Boann.
They'd had hope,
Dill and Kate,
that day.
Please God,
starvation's end.

Dill remembers
Kate's wave,
her form growing smaller
as she moved
farther
and farther away.

The tide was
rising along
the River Boyne Bar.
It took more
than the shoreline.
The tweed of Kate's shawl
had kept walking.
Morning's fog
took her sister away.

Fog hovered
like the shaft
of sunlight
now teasing the stones
of Dill's cell,
brightening the gray
of them,
telling lies.

The stones shiver
or Dill thinks they do.
They wither,
but they don't.
5 ½ feet thick.
Cold as a grave.

She's the only one
awake,
with nothing
but a shadow
in the window
near the ceiling
looking like a face.

Once a Lark, Now a Finch in a Cage

Gravity,
and the finch in the stone cage
of Kilmainham
stays.
No hoist of song.
Lonely,
and only when breath gives out
does a blue chute of air
break the silence.
A double-life creature:
once a life aloft in blue,
all clarity,
now hidden in the swaddle of rock.
Here where,
when summer happens,
no one can see
the long silver ribbons
of a river,
nor hear the song
the bird braids.
Stale air binds earth
to all shadows,
keeps the finch grounded into passages,
dead to song.
Mind-defeated,
she just echoes
a lark
lost in a cave.

All Are One

"The decomposition of the vital organs had anticipated death."
—excerpt from a doctor's report, Cork, winter of 1847

Though only nine years old, Dill knows the stench
of death in the jailcell chamber-pot, knows the moans

of fever from the two sisters everyone calls gypsies,
the Travellers, the 'walking people', the Lucht Siúl.

Caught one night with stones in hand, having broken
into Gravediggers Pub to escape the cold, the rain,

and the ghosts haunting Glasnevin Cemetery, now
they're fighting dysentery—what took Dill's own mother

in so few hours—the 'bloody flux', shock, delirium,
pollution, exhaustion. Their arms are livid, faces haggard.

To each other, the sisters speak Travelers' cant, a language
cryptic and exclusionary. Not to be shared with the buffers.

But Dill and the others know the emergency: a sister's
long, wavy hair, once luxurious, is now caked in shit

able to make them all sick. Dill sees tinkers and peddlers.
These are ones to refuse, to remove. They're restless,

nomadic, seeking refuge on the road. These are itinerant
craftsmen who won't share what's scarce with the evicted.

No different, and yet different—unsettled, untrusting.
Dill knows them as pickpocket, player, and thief.

Then, the jailcell's eldest—the teen—pregnant and sure,
pounds the door for the guard who full-wraps

these sisters in ripped linen sheets, and carts them off
to the fever hut, that wretched cabin for the poor

pitched by the hospital for the poisoned, the scourged,
the unwashed and diseased. And they're never seen again.

The sisters now forced to rest with other Irish in peace—
men, women, and children in one communal grave.

Taken Away

Dill picks the longest pieces
from a hank of straw bedding,

the most sturdy, the most able
to form a leg, an arm, a little doll.

She twists the strands to make
them one body, a friend like the field

sparrow who visits to nibble on crumbs
if any are left. Her brideóg—

the doll's hair sticks out
from every wild angle.

It looks as ragged as Dill.
She has nothing

to paint it a face,
and so that stays blank. Without.

She hides her doll in her corner
beneath threshed straw picked clean

of rat turds and spiders
and heaped for the night like fodder

and silage for livestock.
But soon again, there's a rat

in her haystack—dirty cheese-snatcher—
its whiskers twitching,

mustached
like the garda and the watchman.

It steals her doll
in the clench of its teeth

and carries it away.

Róisín Mac Giolla Bhríghde

The new cell arrival is a pirate, a quiet woman
from the Inishkea Islands, Mayo, off the coast

of Belmullet. So Dill is told. A pagan,
Irish-speaking, worshipping a Godstone

she calls Naomhóg, not Jesus Christ. She'd
robbed boats going west and stolen their cargo.

She's said to have powers over weather and potato,
and her long gray hair is straight, unkempt, and wild.

She wears an amulet at her neck no one would remove.
Dill, and the others, too, back up against the walls

as Róisín—who some call Rose—builds her circle
of little stones and taps her foot over and over

in one chosen spot. She moans and drums her chest—
the heartbeat of the Cailleach. She greets the gateway

to her new life—a world so different—asks protection
from the sidhe who roam the lands and steal

souls away to Mórrígan's cave. Channeling
deity and ancestors, she speaks the lost names

of the dead and turns her eyes to the west,
to a sky against the rising sun, toward eternity.

This, to let them pass—any ghost—to cross them
into heaven, and Dill is suddenly relieved.

Her priest had reported their eviction, had heard
the wailing, knew bodies lay in streets and lanes,

and came despite the famine fever when he could.
But he never gave her father his last rites,

no anointing of the sick, no extreme unction,
nor listened to his last confession to put him

in the state of grace for death. Now
Dill fears he's long-trapped in purgatory, healing

slowly. So, when Róisín burns some bedding straw
with the evening's candle and sends the smoke

through the open window while invoking
names unknown, Dill whispers, *Da, Gerard.*

Remembering

There's a rhythm, a repetition, almost a song—
Dill hears a lone cricket hidden in the shadows.

Eyes closed, it reminds her of home, of before—
four years ago—chicken tucked under her arm

as she walked the hill to her cottage, a single-room
byre, one farm in the clochán. She could smell

Millie the cow come in for winter, remembers
how her father jailed it in the lower end if it cozied

too close to the hearth and chimney, or disturbed
the hard clay floor with its hoof
                    before their evening dancing.

> *A humble scene in a backward place*
> *Where no one important ever looked…*

> *That beautiful, beautiful, beautiful God*
> *Was breathing His love by a cut-away bog.*

Her father'd meant to add a loft one day, to raise the roof,
replace the thatch, secure it with a rope net

and stone ballast. Then, latch the half door—
to lean against, and smoke his pipe, and gossip.

But the potatoes failed, and the landlord's taxes
grew too plentiful. And the whitewash was scoured

off the wattle and daub by fever and loss. Then,
the fire went out, and the people went out,

all gathered on low walls and turf mounds,
and the eggless chickens pecked at the dirt,

endeavoring until they were eaten.

Thomas James O'Connor

Tommy—inmate,
the naughty one caught
pinching the landlord's goat
which had wandered
knee-deep into bog.

He'd killed it. Skinned it.
His sisters ate it with him.
He'd got a hundred-eighty days
hard labor: treadmill,
twenty lashes after solitary—

led down in chains,
down dungeon-stone steps
to the punishment cells.
Two days alone—below
the East Wing into hell.

He's stuttering bravery again now.
Róisín wipes pus from new wounds
on his back, his quivering
chin still beardless at twelve.

She says if he dies his ghost
will haunt these corridors
as surely as Mr. Emmet
haunts the Brazen Head.

Tommy still hears the bleat
of the goat as he steals it.
But it's his own voice now.

Simmering, he listens.
Squinty-eyed and muscle-taut,
he resists. He tests. Twelve,

and once an altar boy,
shapeshifted—

adolescence lost,
childhood become time's fool.

Mary May Flanagan, Inmate

The guard eyes her through the peephole.
A pint of milk for the sake of the baby,
pleads the mother
passing eight months along.

But as he covers the slot, he shouts, *No.*
In his shiny black boots
and coat of brass buttons,
We need it for the stirabout.

First, a deep-throated laugh
that the devil himself must have taught him.

Then, incessant whistling,
and his nightstick slaps his thigh.

The Mary May Flanagan he knows:
pregnant,
unwed,
disgusting,
a whore—
vulgar,
shameless,
indecent,
and sixteen,

caught throwing rocks
at boats laden with oats—
Irish oats meant for England.

She got ninety days incarceration,
and raped again.

Kilmainham's Playground

The children's yard—
there's a chasm of difference
between it and the Kilmainham cells.
Here's a ceiling of blue sky
floored in stone slabs
and a field of gravel.
Three steps and spring—
a hopscotch.
Here, slanting light
sifts into corners,
and catmint survives.
And a finch perches
on stacked boulders to sing
without fear of height,
without its nest.
The weightless thing
on the budding catmint
is a caterpillar—moth's
younger self
destined to spin its wool,
to knit.
All things are born to change their shapes—
even the stonebreakers' stones
cracked smaller and smaller,
now strewn with the confetti
of bitten leaf
and cast cocoons.

Touching Madness

No one should be all alone,
but no one knows this inmate's name.

And no one could explain the riddle
of whatever torments her, the psychosis
or delirium begun months ago.

She's cursed by some devil's messenger
whispering in her ear—some faerie folk
come to steal her soul—and so,

she squats alone in the rocky corner
of the children's yard, picking nits.

Boys walk clockwise, girls counter-
clockwise, all eyes to the ground,

circling, and the repetition of it
gives this girl peace. Foundling, beggar,

she still extends one hand and hopes
for a rind of turnip or the core
of a discarded apple to suck.

The jailer finds her miserable—
idiot—criminal—sin. He promises
she'll end up in the Lunatic Asylum.

When exercise-time is finally done,
Dill's the one who taps each finger
of the waif's outstretched hand

and guides the unbalanced girl
like a shepherd with a lame one in his herd.

No one should ever be alone.
Dill had a crippled kitten once.
Its mother left it outside the pig-shed.

Twelve Lashes for Dill

for guiding the simpleton /
for the audacity /
to lift her eyes /
to the sky as if asking /
for God's forgiveness /
undeserved—so denied /
twelve lashes /
to prepare the child /
for reform /
for her crime /
debt, pauper, theft, hunger /
for having life /

Mary Soothes Dill as She Sleeps

In her dream, Dill's changed into the village sheep
beside her mother's spinning wheel, giving up

its wool straight off its back—no shearing,
no squabble with the blades—she gives

willingly, long threads pulled from her
soft chest leaving budding breasts exposed,

more naked with each unraveling spin.
She fears she'll soon be down to spine and gristle.

In the name of whatever's holy, she doesn't know
what she'll become. Mary covers the restless

Dill with their only blanket, thin and rough. Then,
in her dream, there are bluebells on a river's edge,

the soft of moss, the hum of Drogheda, pots
bubbling on a banked fire that no one must attend.

The river waters cast no shadows—only wonder,
and they're full of salmon. A ledge serves as an altar,

blessings bestowed and all sins forgiven.
In her dream, her mother slips warm selkie skin

on her shivering body, a sacred sweater knitted
from her own good wool now changing into feathers

—wings—and the chaffinch in the hedge grows
jealous with the melody of her singing. Purple

foxgloves stretch heavenward, sky an eggshell blue.
The lark learns to weave its nest with the silk of a spider.

Punishment: Picking Oakum

Men ax junk ship-rope into shorter lengths, beat
the rigging with mallet and cudgel to break up
creosote and pine pitch. They drop pound
after pound at Dill's feet to pick and unravel
what's worn and useless, to loosen, tease, and twist
its threads with fingers black and bloodied.

First, she tears apart the shank's corkscrewed entrails
and rolls each strand across her knee.
Then she scratches at it until there's nothing left
but tuft. Tuft to become wads and padding—to caulk

planks and seams and cracks of worthy ships. Or,
it will be bandages meant for the sick and wounded,
for their bedding mats, or for the cloth of uniforms.

Sentenced:
Pounds of oakum—five hours a day—for a week
in total silence: *Remember why you're here.*

You'll earn your keep, or you'll die trying.

Judged:
      a tarred rope

      stripped
of dignity,
         humiliated,

        shamed

to inner strength:

    the bast
    of hemp

in her
fingers.

A Charm of Finches

From a distance, through the window,
the cellmates' music can be heard,
and it is beautiful—full of what pleases:

their drum-pulse against a tin dinner plate,
a bodhrán never-the-less, connecting
hard time with the rhythm of the day.

Róisín and Dill play in harmony,
Tommy's pucker-cheeked whistle
keeping up—a melody for wandering.

Mary hums as she sways with the baby
jumping in her womb. A happy day.

Then, quickly, as if hunting the hedges
for the Wren Day wren, the warden
rummages through their soggy straw

and filters out their stick cipín, the tipper
which keeps the time. Then, too, he takes
their empty battered dinner plate.

And he can try and try and try to kill,
but these cellmates will
sing as one—a charm of finches who

tap together now with fingers and thumbs
on limestone walls and thighs. He'll never stop
the heartbeat of their chorus which asks,

How long must we sing this song?

The Chaplain Teaches the Alphabet

Dill's finger draws through dry sand—
each granule parts a path and leaves
her mark—A for Absolution,

for Abysmal, Assault, Asylum,
Accident, Animal—for Ann.

Two N's seem a gluttonous sin,
but sounds double-down to make sure—
Name, Number, Nothing,
No way to find her Kate.

With practice, slate-on-slate, more
permanent, still able to remove, to erase—

a swipe of the hand and the stone
is cleared as if nothing was ever
there—like ablution—a disappearance.

She hears: Derelict, Drunkard, Discard, Done.
She sets her chin defiantly, learns

how to spell *live*, so close to *alive*,
and speaks Daring, Durable, Dill.

From Rascal to the Barque *Royal Meridian*

Caught gambling in the schoolyard,
Tommy's sun-red hair flames the cell,
his temper keeping up with it.

Never idle, never quiet, he's a bundle
of willow on fire. With the strength of oak,
he chisels the wall using bullet-hard flint:

1851 + Done
graffiti which gets him confinement again
for defacing public property: 2 days solitary.

And when he shivs the guard
across the thick of his arm—hanging
snarls as possible until the final verdict's

heard: transportation—a convict ship
to Van Diemen's Land, Australia,
9 years for the goat and all the spailpín trouble.

Shackled in leg iron and chain,
Tommy joins thief, burglar, and prostitute,
the obscene, corrupt, and disobedient,

all decently poor seeking moral reform
clustered together on the dock and the gangplank,
blowing kisses good-bye to a homeland forever.

Cian Mac Giolla Bhríghde Visits Róisín

He wouldn't say where he got the money
but he'd had enough to pay off
the sentry—to let him in to see Róisín,
his mother, one last time before he sailed
west into New York's oyster harbor.

He'd aged. He says he couldn't leave without
holding her again, without giving her
the skirts and shawls his wife and daughter wore
before they went with God—why
now he's off somewhere so unfamiliar.

The Young Rebellion, that battle
at Widow McCormack's cabbage patch,
had failed. Now, whispers of another movement.
They call themselves the Fenians, he says, and Róisín
knows there's no sense arguing, no sense

denying his temper now he's made up his mind.
Then, when the plodding warden unbolts the door,
she watches her son grow to a ghost in the shadows,
and hands the dresses to Mary and Dill—
optimistic clothes mended and patched as necessary.

Annunciation

It's a gentle lamb-rain
blows through the cell window,
a cloud-angel come
to visit her, a messenger
of holy water
like on the tidal flat
where periwinkles
could be gathered
while laughing at a gull.

Dill lifts her face,
stares at the vaulted opening:
a scissure in the body
of block-stone.
She almost feels the spray
of Atlantic waves
flung against
the bone-stark rock.

She tastes the salt
and licks sea-brine:
the tears of creation.
These waters of Emmanuel
say God is with us still
here at Mary's Well.

Mary May Flanagan Gives Birth

Any light in the cell has been rinsed
of its ambition, and yet anticipation

still hangs as hopeful as wet fog in a drought.
Labor—and this is when the bitter herbs

and roots hand-searched by Róisín
may have eased the pain, but in Kilmainham

there are none. Mary groans, mad in the dark.
Straw-sprawled, shiver-moaning,

she claws open the gate Eve promised,
intense and earnest, penitent

and bargaining with God—peddling
with makeshift prayers as useful as

shoveling the bog with a dull turf blade.
Spark to flame to bonfire rabid,

her sweat and blood chokes the small
room until one round head delivers itself

to a world walled in gray stone. The mother
wails one long note. Then, a wretched gasp

escapes the pirate-midwife who covers the child
and his open-cleft spine with the threadbare rags

of Mary's dirty skirt, and whispers, *Defect.*
Monstrous...Fomhórach born into this cave.

The Gartan Mother's Lullaby

—Herbert Hughes and Seosamh Mac Cathmhaoil

~~"Sleep, O babe, for the red bee hums~~
~~The silent twilight's fall~~
~~Aoibheall from~~ the Grey Rock ~~comes~~
~~To wrap the world in thrall.~~
~~A leanbhan O, my child, my joy,~~
~~My love and heart's desire,~~
~~The crickets sing you lullaby~~
Beside the dying ~~fire.~~

~~Dusk is drawn, and the Green Man's Thorn~~
~~Is~~ wreathed ~~in rings of fog:~~
~~Siabhra sails his boat till morn~~
~~Upon the Starry Bog.~~
~~A leanbhan O, the paly moon~~
~~Hath brimmed her cusp in dew,~~
~~And weeps to hear the sad sleep-tune~~
~~I sing, O love, to you.~~

~~Faintly sweet doth the chapel bell~~
~~Ring o'er~~ the valley dim:
~~Tearmann's peasant-voices swell~~
~~In fragrant evening hymn.~~
~~A leanbhan O, the low bell rings~~
~~My little lamb to rest~~
~~And angel-dreams, till morning sings~~
~~Its music in your breast."~~

Dill strikes all music from her breast
and keens what's left:

    The grey rock
    beside the dying
    wreathed
    the valley dim.

Christening

The priest asks, "What name is given this child?"
and Mary says, "John. John Joseph Flanagan."
So, before contagion and the maggots can set in,
and death can mercifully take him, John receives
the Sign of the Cross, with Dill, his godmother,
holding him in her arms and folding a ragged bit
of linen over his eyes to shield him from devils
circling these ruins, having settled in the weakest,
full-lodged, who suddenly release their grasp as
John slides into garden-bliss of Christ's anointed.

No Choice for the Impoverished

She'd heard the stories
of anatomy burials—
decaying, broken
corpses and cadavers
of those too poor
to pay for funerals;
claims of *anatomical examination*,
of body parts traded
and sold in pieces—
the un-named
staged for professionals.
There's competition
for the diseased,
deformed,
for birth defects
—to learn,
they say—
explorations denying resurrection
to the destitute.
One last time,
Mary touches
eyelash, eyelid, curl,
and kisses his lips
now free from indigence
and suffering.
Hands her baby,
little finch,
to Kilmainham's matron.

The Spiderweb

It's the way the mist beads
on the filaments in the upper
corner which catches Dill's eye.
The interlocking spiral,
deceivingly beautiful, is made
recognizable. It glitters clearly.

The spider's lived there beyond
Dill's reach, descending now
and then on a single silk
strand finer than the whisker
on an ant, nearly as invisible.
Fast as the flying shuttle of a loom.

He dangles without knowing
where he's going, leaving
his safe place to visit her,
to say hello, to parachute
with his eight legs, all necessary.
Dill's learned to count them:
four plus four makes eight,

same number of days before
Mary leaves, still bleeding,
for the workhouse. Freed to go
with no place to go, no
other home to go to. That place—
a ragged, undignified misery,
a trap made with strands of iron.

This spider's web of spit belongs
to Kilmainham stones and will
remain, will try to collect more
pearly jewels of dew as well as
innocent intruders—small gnats
risking the sticky tangles as they try
to fill their empty bellies.

Mórrígan in Kilmainham

Róisín, Dill, and Mary
wrap in each other's arms.
The crow of battle cannot be caged,
the pagan witch explains.
I am
a hag full of dreams,
pulled along these stones
on pointed elbows,
imprisoned here forever,
and yet,
I will go forth
embodied in you.

We are
crone, mother, maiden—
the triple goddess, Mórrígan.

Chant our messages.
Shriek and stir the fight.
We are
spirits of the fertile women.
We are one.
Three women's blood now mixed.
And we will
feed whatever comes next.
When the winds die down,
every Irish bird
wherever flown
will have drunk the milk of us.

Mary Goes to the Poorhouse

She sees a dozen die of plague each day,
carted to the pit, some still alive,
some dropped through slip-bottom coffins,

most dropped to the bottom of a trench.

Deemed unclean and less than a perfect woman,
Mary labors in the laundry, a lingering
wither, but the Irish crowbar-brigades

with muscled horses yoked in rope & pulley
had levelled so many homes,
had set fire to thatched roofs, and left

nothing to return to, and so she must endure.

At least, she has more than a winnowing
sheet above her head. Tells herself to be
industrious—not fodder for the body snatchers,
not slunk into the madness of a lunatic.

She resolves to slop the uniforms soaking
in stone tubs, to scrub raw with the washboard
and the dolly stick, scald herself in boiling

water, be burned with soap made of ashes, lye,
and fat. She's determined to retrieve

the skirt and knitted shawl Cian gifted her,
now fumigated and waiting to be worn

one day when she's not called a 'fallen woman',
when her shaved head of curls regrows—redeemed.

Mary May Flanagan—she wouldn't let them
change her name. She would learn a trade.
But today, she folds prison shirts in silence

for oatmeal, sour milk and tea, and sometimes,
bread, boiled mutton on a Sunday.

Forced to Witness an Inmate's Hanging

Nobody knows who he is.
The sky can be so purple blackbirds disappear.
Clouds are either ghosts or angels.
A girl who walks barefoot pummels nothing.
Rubble in the courtyard cuts her callused heels.
No one cares about stubbed toes.
Dill is hauled to the courtyard to watch.
She doesn't know who he is.
Raw wind has eyes when it wants to.
A condemned man makes the sign of the cross.
His hands are tied behind his back.
The Hangman's Walk connects chapel to doorway.
A man walks slowly on some paths.
Convicts hang in public.
She's forced to watch with eyes wide open.
No man is nobody.
The balcony is not as high as clouds.
Clouds can carry either ghosts or angels.
Purple blackbirds gather when they want to.
Fear never smells of apple cider or honeysuckle.
Footsteps on a ladder drum like falling rocks.
She's forced to watch.
A finch stops singing when the death bell rings.
The sky can only do so much.

Uisneach on Bealtaine

Peas   jacketed on the vine
        chill   in darkness   ripen.

Like so many   fireflies   sparks
            enter the world.

Embers   fire: primitive light
                            breath-origin
                        ancestor.

A Spell for Dill's Emancipation

As first mate of the square-sailed *Servant's Revenge*,
Róisín had seen kidnap, ambush, raid, and wild escape,
but she knows she'll die in this jail. Life sentence.
Faces of the dead have stared at her. Nothing to fear.

Soon released, Dill stares as uncertain as a ghost lost in fog,
—the yellow fog that rubs its back upon the window-panes,
the yellow smoke that rubs its muzzle—and can smother.
Róisín's foghorn call: *Go away. Go. Your time is up.*

Dill has sent a letter to Mary—no poorhouse for Dill, no
more picking oakum. And Róisín can recognize courage.
She renames Dill—Áine, goddess, the spark of life,

the summer sun, the red mare, and bloodstone's blood.
Tells Dill she descends from the Lady of the Lake—Áine.
Say her name, Ann Gallagher, for it's your own.

*

Kilmainham's iron gates open to liberate
those whose sentence ends today: the burglar, thief,
prostitute, beggar, vagrant, huckster, pickpocket

—and Dill—standing on the cobblestones. Stunned,
she hears Mary,
    I've come for you. No poorhouse for the two of us.

She promises to search for Kate. Search always
and forevermore. Because no one should be all alone.
And Dill asks,
    Áine. Could you call me Áine now?

remembering Róisín's last good-bye—

Gather bee balm and angelica,
cowslip, mugwort, elder, goat's rue,
nettle, fennel, flax.

It all belongs to you.
A bit of mistletoe and bladderwrack,
sweet lavender's protection.

When you leave this prison cell,
breathe deeply,
once, thrice, many times.

Let the sunrays warm you,
sink into your skin, Ann Gallagher.
Draw its heat into your heart,

the middle cauldron of your motion.
See its ball of fire. Fill
your body with its light.

Look into Áine's eyes,
then back out through your own.
What can never be taken away.

Invoke your true name—say it—
                              Áine.

Notes

"The Great Hunger"
An Gorta Mór means The Great Hunger in Irish.
Stirabout is a porridge made from oatmeal or cornmeal stirred into boiling water.

"The Gallagher Family"
The bean sí (anglicized, banshee) is the "woman of the faerie mound," a spirit in Irish mythology who wails to herald the death of a family member. The phrase, *what had once been a man*, is from a witness report of the Justice of the Peace, N.M. Cummings, from Cork.

"Into Kilmainham's West Wing"
A triskele is the ancient motif of three conjoined spirals often found carved into the megalithic tombs such as Newgrange in Ireland.

"Once a Lark, Now a Finch in a Cage"
With deep gratitude to the poet, this poem is based on an erasure of "Lark-Luster" by Eamon Grennan which can be found at:
www.poetryfoundation.org/poetrymagazine/poems/150747/lark-luster

"Róisín Mac Giolla Bhríghde"
Due to the lack of jail space in Kilmainham Gaol at the time, adults (men and women) and children were all housed together in one cell when necessary.
In Irish mythology, the sidhe are faerie-folk themselves or the faerie-mounds in which they live.
The Cailleach is the "Divine Hag" associated with the creation of the landscape and weather, especially winter.
The Mórrígan is the "Great Queen" thought to be a shapeshifting trio of women associated with warfare and fate, especially foretelling death.

"Remembering"
A clochán is a hamlet or small village in Irish, more specifically the stepping stones of a ford.
With deep gratitude to the poet, the lines in italics are from "The One" by Patrick Kavanagh which can be found at www.onbeing.org/poetry/the-one/

"Thomas James O'Connor"
Robert Emmet (1778-1803) was an Irish Republican rebel who was
hanged and beheaded for high treason following an uprising against the
Crown.
The Brazen Head is a pub in the Merchant's Quay quarter of Dublin which
has been in business since the 1660s and which was frequented by Robert
Emmet.

"Kilmainham's Playground"
The line, *All things are born to change their shapes*, is the title of a book of
poetry by Jennifer Martelli, Small Harbor Publishing, 2023, in which she
cites this as from Ovid's *Metamorphosis*.

"Mary Soothes Dill as She Sleeps"
In Irish and Scottish mythology, the selkie is a water creature which can
shapeshift between seal and human forms by wearing or removing its
sealskin.

"A Charm of Finches"
Wren Day, also known as St. Stephen's Day (December 26), involves the
tradition of hunting a wren, and then while dressed in masks and straw
clothes, the wrenboys (aka, mummers) go from house-to-house collecting
pennies. The wren was considered a symbol of the past year.
The line, *How long must we sing this song?* is from the song, *Sunday
Bloody Sunday*, by Bono, U2.

"From Rascal to the Barque *Royal Meridian*"
The word spailpín means *rascal* in Irish and refers to the wandering,
landless laborers and itinerant Irish workers enduring hard physical labor,
low wages, and mistreatment by landowners.

"Cian Mac Giolla Bhríghde Visits Róisín"
The Fenians were an oath-bound secret society for the Irish Republican
Brotherhood and their brethren in America dedicated to the independence
of the Irish Republic. Its mythological roots include nomadic warrior
bands of young nobles who would leave their society, then return to inherit
their titles as kings and queens.

"Annunciation"
The name Emmanuel means "God is with us."
Mary's Well is "the spring of the Virgin Mary" where, in Christianity, the

Archangel Gabriel appeared to Mary, the mother of Jesus, to announce that she would bear the son of God.

"Mary May Flanagan Gives Birth"
Fomhórach (anglicized, Fomorians) are monstrous beings in Irish mythology thought to be hostile to the first settlers of Ireland. They represent the wild, destructive powers of nature and personify chaos and death.

"The Garten Mother's Lullaby"
The lyrics were written in 1904 and the song can be heard at:
www.youtube.com/watch?v=O0PkDqNF7-Y.

Aoibheall is the queen of the Northern Faeries.
The Green Man (*Fear Glas* in Irish) is said to do nothing to you in the morning, but if seen at night, misfortune will overcome you.
Siabhra is a generic term for an Irish faerie.
Tearmann is a village near Gartan in Donegal.
Leanbhan means *little child* in Irish.

"Mary Goes to the Poorhouse"
The crowbar brigades were agents of large English estates, often desperate Irishmen paid with food, who would tear down and burn homes of the Irish evicted from the lands.

"Uisneach on Bealtaine"
The Hill of Uisneach is a sacred neolithic sanctuary in the midlands of Ireland, first excavated in the 1920s and thought to be a gateway to the mythical otherworld. This "hill-portal" can be linked to the concept of the hill-mounds of the faerie folk.
Bealtaine is the day (around May 1) midway between the spring equinox and the summer solstice of the northern hemisphere. It marks the beginning of summer and is celebrated by the lighting of fires. On this day, it's thought the veil between this world and the faerie world is especially porous.

"A Spell for Dill's Emancipation"
The lines, 'The yellow fog that rubs its back upon the window-panes, / The yellow smoke that rubs its muzzle', are from "The Love Song of J. Alfred Prufrock" by T.S. Eliot.

About the Author

D. WALSH GILBERT is the author of five poetry collections: *Ransom* and *imagine the small bones* (both, Grayson Books), *Once the Earth had Two Moons* (Cerasus Poetry), *[M]AR[Y]* (Kelsay Books), and *Deirdre* (Impspired).

A multiple Pushcart Prize nominee and winner of *The Ekphrastic Review*'s 2021 "Bird Watching" contest, her work has recently appeared in *The Inflectionist Review*, *The Field Guide Poetry Magazine*, *The Lumiere Review*, *Black Fox Literary Magazine*, and *New Feathers Anthology*, among others. She serves on the board of the non-profit Riverwood Poetry Series, and as co-editor of *Connecticut River Review*, published by the Connecticut Poetry Society.

She lives in Farmington, Connecticut on a former sheep farm at the foot of Talcott Mountain, previously the homeland of the Tunxis peoples and near the oldest site of human occupation in Connecticut, dating back 12,500 years. She welcomes wildlife daily from the forest behind her home and writes every day. A dual citizen of Ireland and the United States of America, she visits her homelands in County Monaghan as often as she can.